THE STORY OF THE
ATLANTA
HAWKS

CREATIVE EDUCATION

Published by Creative Education
123 South Broad Street
Mankato, Minnesota 56001
Creative Education is an imprint of The Creative Company.

DESIGN AND PRODUCTION BY **EVANSDAY DESIGN**

PHOTOGRAPHS BY Getty Images (Andrew D. Bernstein / NBAE,
Nathaniel S. Butler / NBAE, Scott Cunningham / NBAE, Tim DeFrisco,
Stephen Dunn, Focus on Sport, Walter Iooss Jr. / NBAE, Jed
Jacobsohn / Allsport, Fernando Medina / NBAE, NBA Photos, NBAE,
Wen Roberts, Noren Trotman / NBAE, Rocky Widner / NBAE)

Copyright © 2007 Creative Education.
International copyright reserved in all countries.
No part of this book may be reproduced in any form
without written permission from the publisher.
Printed in the United States of America

LIBRARY OF CONGRESS CATALOGING-IN-PUBLICATION DATA

LeBoutillier, Nate.
The story of the Atlanta Hawks / by Nate LeBoutillier.
p. cm. — (The NBA: a history of hoops)
Includes index.
ISBN-13: 978-1-58341-399-9
1. Atlanta Hawks (Basketball team)—History—
Juvenile literature. I. Title. II. Series.

GV885.52.A7L43 2006
796.323'64'09758231—dc22   2005050033

First edition

9 8 7 6 5 4 3 2 1

COVER PHOTO: *Marvin Williams*

THE STORY OF THE
ATLANTA HAWKS

NATE LeBOUTILLIER

CREATIVE EDUCATION

In Atlanta, Georgia,

THE AIR CAN HANG HEAVY WITH MOISTURE. BUT ABOVE A BASKETBALL COURT, A MAN FLOATS ABOVE HIS OPPONENTS, A BASKETBALL OUTSTRETCHED IN HIS RIGHT HAND. THE MAN WEARS A UNIFORM OF WHITE, RED, AND GOLD WITH THE NUMBER 21 EMBLAZONED ON IT. HE SEEMS TO HANG FOREVER IN THE AIR, FLOATING IMPOSSIBLY. FINALLY, AS HE NEARS THE BASKET, HE REARS BACK AND COCKS THE BALL LIKE A SLINGSHOT. HIS ARM SNAPS OUT AS THE SLINGSHOT RELEASES, SENDING THE BALL CRASHING THROUGH THE RIM. NOT MANY COULD FLY AS HIGH AS DOMINIQUE WILKINS.

HAWKS TAKE FLIGHT

FOUNDED IN THE 1830S, ATLANTA, GEORGIA, WAS BUILT at the southern tip of the Appalachian Mountains. By the start of the Civil War, Atlanta had become a stronghold of the Confederate army. In 1864, the Union army captured the young city and burned it to ashes. Gradually, the city was rebuilt with pride and toil. Today, Atlanta is home to a professional basketball team that has had its share of glorious triumphs and terrible defeats as well. That team, the Atlanta Hawks of the National Basketball Association (NBA), was born in 1949.

The Hawks franchise was originally known as the Tri-City Blackhawks, one of the NBA's 17 original teams. The team was shared by three neighboring cities: Rock Island, Illinois; Moline, Illinois; and Davenport, Iowa. The Blackhawks spent two mediocre seasons in the Tri-Cities and then four in Milwaukee, Wisconsin, before owner Ben Kerner moved his team again in 1955, this time to St. Louis, Missouri. The city seemed to bring good luck to the franchise at last.

Early star Bob Pettit's hardworking approach helped make him a two-time NBA Most Valuable Player (MVP)

HOOPS

NBA

Famous for his hook shot, forward Cliff Hagan scored 26 points in a single quarter in one 1958 game

The Hawks were led by a 6-foot-9 and 240-pound forward named Bob Pettit. Pettit was drafted out of Louisiana State University in 1954 and had an immediate impact on the league, earning NBA Rookie of the Year honors and emerging as the Hawks' first true superstar. In his second season, Pettit averaged 25 points and 16 rebounds per game to earn the league's Most Valuable Player (MVP) award.

By the late '50s, the Hawks had surrounded Pettit with much talent, and players such as forwards Cliff Hagan and Ed Macauley gave the team the look of a champion. In 1957, St. Louis drove all the way to the NBA Finals, only to lose to the powerful Boston Celtics in seven hard-fought games. But the next season, the Hawks defeated the Celtics four games to two in the NBA Finals, with Pettit scoring an incredible 50 points in the sixth game—a 110–109 win—to seal the franchise's first and only championship. "It was the highlight of my 11-year professional career, no doubt," said Pettit years later. "It's something that you look back on forever."

PISTOL PETE

Pete Maravich, an Atlanta Hawks star guard from 1970 to 1974, was at his best when he was just having fun. Most players take games very seriously, but "Pistol Pete" had no problem with throwing a tricky, behind-the-back pass here or bouncing a whirling, between-the-legs dribble there—he'd been doing it all his life. Maravich could dribble at age three and spin a basketball on his finger at age eight. On January 5, 1988, in a Pasadena, California, gym, Maravich died while playing the game he loved. Having just finished a pick-up game, the 40-year-old Maravich told another player, "I need to do this more often. I'm really feeling good." Then he dropped to the floor with a heart attack and died. Many people said that a basketball court was where Pistol Pete would've wanted to die.

ON TO ATLANTA

THE HAWKS REMAINED A CONTENDER THROUGH THE early 1960s. New stars such as point guard Lenny Wilkens and bruising center Clyde Lovellette were added to the lineup, but the team never regained the championship magic of 1958. After the 1964–65 season, Pettit retired. Then, in 1968, Ben Kerner decided to sell the team to a group of Atlanta businessmen. The sale came as a shock to both cities, but Kerner felt that St. Louis could no longer compete financially as an NBA market.

Famous for his wild hair and amazing passes, Pete Maravich was among Atlanta's first stars

Known for his versatile skills, high-scoring forward John Drew (pictured) starred alongside Lou Hudson

The move to Atlanta was made smoother by the emergence of young star Lou Hudson. Nicknamed "Sweet Lou" by teammates and fans, the 6-foot-5 forward was an expert marksman from all over the court. "As soon as Lou steps in the gym, he's in range," joked Hawks forward Bill Bridges.

Hudson averaged more than 18 points a game his rookie year. Starting in 1968–69, Sweet Lou then led the Hawks to the playoffs for five straight seasons. But despite Hudson's efforts and those of other great players such as forwards John Drew and Zelmo Beaty and guards Walt Hazzard and Pete Maravich, the Hawks could not get past the second round of postseason play.

Part of the problem was that Atlanta kept losing talented players to the rival American Basketball Association (ABA). "We'd just get a good bunch together and then we'd lose one or two of them," complained Hawks coach Richie Guerin after losing Beaty and high-scoring guard Joe "Pogo" Caldwell in successive seasons.

After the Boston Celtics eliminated the Hawks in the second round of the 1973 playoffs, Atlanta's postseason run was over. Four straight losing seasons followed, leaving fans with little to cheer about except Hudson's scoring exploits. Sweet Lou led the charge until 1977, when he was traded to the Los Angeles Lakers.

The losing seasons of the mid-1970s were hard on the Hawks franchise, and it was widely rumored that the Hawks would be forced to move yet again. All talk of another move was put to rest in January 1977, however, when Ted Turner, a wealthy media mogul, bought the Hawks and stabilized their position in Atlanta.

With the Hawks' financial problems behind them, the team's fortunes began to rise. In the 1977 NBA Draft, Atlanta chose 7-foot-1 and 250-pound center Wayne "Tree" Rollins. The towering Rollins gave the team a fearsome defensive presence under the basket. "Tree is the type of guy you hope to have around for 10 years," noted Hawks coach Hubie Brown. "He has a great work ethic and gives you everything he has every night."

MASTER COACH With a 22-point Hawks win over the Washington Bullets on January 6, 1995, coach Lenny Wilkens became the NBA's all-time leader in coaching victories, with 939. Wilkens coached the Hawks from 1993 to 2000, earning a combined record of 310–232. Wilkens also coached the Portland Trail Blazers, Seattle SuperSonics, Cleveland Cavaliers, Toronto Raptors, and New York Knicks, piling up a 1,332–1,155 career record. Wilkens was no slouch as a player either (he played for the Hawks from 1960 to 1968 and for three other teams), scoring 17,772 career points. He is today a member of the Basketball Hall of Fame as both a coach and a player. "He's poised, calm, and patient, always under control, accepting the good and the bad equally," said former NBA coach Jack Ramsay, another Basketball Hall-of-Famer.

ATLANTA HAWKS

Tree Rollins was one of the most fearsome shot blockers in NBA history, piling up 2,542 career blocks

HAWKS FIND THEIR 'NIQUE

THE 1977–78 HAWKS POSTED AN IMPROVED 41–41 record and made a return to the playoffs but were quickly eliminated by the Washington Bullets. As the 1980s began, Rollins, guard Charlie Criss, and forward Dan Roundfield formed the core of some solid Atlanta teams. But they lacked the scoring punch necessary to win big playoff games.

Dan Roundfield routinely posted double-digit nightly totals in points and rebounds in the early '80s

ATLANTA HAWKS

19

Doc Rivers ran Atlanta's offense with a leadership that would later make him a successful NBA coach

On September 3, 1982, the Hawks made a trade with the Utah Jazz for the draft rights to University of Georgia standout Dominique Wilkins, giving them the offensive star they had been lacking. During his college career, the high-flying Wilkins had earned the nickname "The Human Highlight Film" for his thrill-a-minute style and sensational dunks. In his rookie year, the 6-foot-8 and 215-pound forward averaged 17 points a game.

To support Wilkins, Atlanta coach Mike Fratello added impressive performers such as guards Anthony "Spud" Webb and Glenn "Doc" Rivers and muscular power forward Kevin Willis. In 1986–87, this new Hawks lineup posted a franchise-best 57–25 record. Leading the way was Wilkins, who finished second in the league in scoring with 29 points a game. "I think we will go as far as Dominique will carry us," said Fratello.

In the 1987 playoffs, the Hawks soared past the Indiana Pacers in the first round to earn a showdown with the Detroit Pistons and their star point guard, Isiah Thomas. The two Eastern Conference powers slugged it out for five games, but the Hawks came up short.

THE LITTLEST HAWK

Many kids dream of the day they will play in the big game, in front of a big crowd. They imagine what it would look like if they were on the court against the giants that play in the NBA. Well, kids got a glimpse of what this would look like when Anthony "Spud" Webb joined the Hawks in 1985. Standing only 5-foot-7, weighing 130 pounds, and wearing a babyfaced look, Webb looked a bit like a kid out there. But he was as quick as a waterbug and could dart under, around, and between bigger players before they knew what had happened. And Webb had another weapon: superhero-like leaping ability. Despite his short stature, he could dunk the basketball, and even won the NBA's Slam Dunk Contest in his rookie season.

The next season, Coach Fratello guided the Hawks to another 50-win season, and again his team battled into the second round of the playoffs. This time Atlanta's opponent was the Boston Celtics. Fans were treated to a thrilling show as Wilkins and Celtics star Larry Bird staged a classic shootout, but in the end, the Celtics triumphed.

Wilkins's Human Highlight Film continued its run in Atlanta through the 1993–94 season, when the Hawks decided to rebuild. In February 1994, Atlanta traded Wilkins to the Los Angeles Clippers. Wrote basketball journalist Lang Whitaker: "That trade ruined pro basketball in Atlanta. You can make bad trades, you make trades that set a franchise back a few years, or you can make moves that completely ruin a sport in a city. Atlanta lost their only NBA hero, and from then on things plummeted downhill."

THE DUEL On May 22, 1988, the Hawks and the Boston Celtics met in Boston for one of the best playoff Game 7s in NBA history. The Hawks had taken a three-games-to-two lead in the second-round series, but the Celtics somehow survived elimination in Game 6 with a two-point win. Game 7 saw the Hawks' Dominique Wilkins lock horns with Celtics star Larry Bird. Wilkins ended up with 47 points on several powerful dunks and high-flying shots, while Bird fired his way to 34 points. But Bird saved 20 of those 34 points for the fourth quarter alone, and the Celtics won the game, 118–116, and the series. "The game turned into such a two-man shootout," said *Sports Illustrated* journalist Jack McCallum, "that it's known as 'The Bird and Dominique Game.' Dominique Wilkins was never better."

ATLANTA HAWKS

An electrifying offensive force, Dominique Wilkins appeared in nine straight NBA All-Star Games

23

FROM MUTOMBO TO WILLIAMS

ALTHOUGH THE HAWKS CERTAINLY WEREN'T "ruined," they did need to retool their lineup. Guards Steve Smith and Mookie Blaylock took center stage in Atlanta's revamped attack in the mid-1990s. Despite the leadership of new coach Lenny Wilkens, the team struggled when it came to the playoffs. Year after year, the Hawks' lack of a talented big man left them vulnerable to inside attacks. "Championship teams start from the inside out," noted Wilkens. "We need a stronger presence down low in order to contend."

ATLANTA HAWKS

Mookie Blaylock was a great passer and star defender, leading the league in steals in 1996–97 and 1997–98

25

Dikembe Mutombo reigned as the NBA's number-one shot blocker for a remarkable five straight seasons

Wilkens got his wish in 1996 when the Hawks signed veteran center Dikembe Mutombo. The 7-foot-2 and 260-pound Mutombo had already established himself as one of the game's most daunting shot blockers and rebounders. In his first five seasons with the Denver Nuggets, Mutombo had averaged more than 12 points, 12 rebounds, and 3 blocked shots a game. "He's an intimidator," said forward Alan Henderson, another new addition to the Atlanta lineup. "Now he's our intimidator."

"Mount Mutombo" instantly improved the Hawks. Still, three straight winning seasons were followed by three early exits in the playoffs. The Hawks were again tough defensively, but they now lacked offensive punch. In 1999, both Smith and Blaylock left the team. A year later, the Hawks dropped to 28–54.

The Hawks' next six seasons, from 1999–00 to 2004–05, were rough. The team went a combined 162–330, finishing dead last in its division four times. The 2004–05 season was the worst yet, as Atlanta finished at the bottom of the entire NBA with a 13–69 record.

HAWKS DUNKERS DOMINATE

What is it about the Atlanta Hawks and the All-Star weekend Slam Dunk Contest? Is there some jumping potion added to Atlanta's drinking water? Hawks dunking domination started the day before the 1985 All-Star Game in Indianapolis when Dominique "The Human Highlight Film" Wilkins captured the dunk contest with his famous windmill and tomahawk jams. The next year, little Spud Webb soared above even Wilkins to take the title. Wilkins won again in 1990 to give the Hawks their third dunk title in six years. In 2005, the next great Hawks dunker took flight. His name was Josh Smith, and he wowed fans with his superball-style leaping ability and brought the dunk title back to Atlanta. As an added touch, Smith wore Wilkins's old number 21 jersey during one of his winning dunks.

The forecast in Atlanta was looking up, though, as the Hawks picked up two promising players in the 2005 NBA Draft: Marvin Williams, an explosive, 6-foot-8 forward, and Salim Stoudemire, a guard with a knack for hitting clutch shots. The Hawks counted on Williams and Stoudemire to mesh with other up-and-coming young players such as lanky forwards Josh Smith and Josh Childress. "I want to win," Williams said after being drafted by Atlanta. "Everybody wants to win. We're all going to work hard, we're going to be young, but at least we're going to learn the game of basketball from the coaches."

For more than 50 years, the Hawks have been one of the NBA's most colorful franchises, led by dynamic stars such as the rim-rocking Dominique Wilkins. They have enjoyed moments of glory, including one league title, and they have suffered setbacks. Now, after some low times, today's Hawks plan to again fly to championship heights.

ATLANTA

HAWKS

Marvin Williams played just one college season (University of North Carolina) before entering the NBA

Fans hoped that sensational dunker Josh Smith would help the Hawks fly to championship heights

INDEX

A
American Basketball Association 15
Atlanta Hawks
    first season 8
    relocations 8, 12
    team records 21

B
Basketball Hall of Fame 16
Beaty, Zelmo 15
Blaylock, Mookie 24, **25**, 27
Bridges, Bill 15
Brown, Hubie 16

C
Caldwell, Joe ("Pogo") 15
Childress, Josh 28
Criss, Charlie 18

D
Davenport, Iowa 8
Drew, John **14**, 15

F
Fratello, Mike 21, 22

G
Guerin, Richie 15

H
Hagan, Cliff **10**, 11
Hazzard, Walt 15
Henderson, Alan 27
Hudson, Lou 15

K
Kerner, Ben 8, 12

L
Lovellette, Clyde 12

M
Macauley, Ed 11
Maravich, Pete 11, **11**, **13**, 15
Milwaukee, Wisconsin 8
Moline, Illinois 8
Most Valuable Player Award 11
Mutombo, Dikembe **26**, 27

N
NBA championship 11, 28
NBA Finals 11
NBA playoffs 11, 15, 18, 21, 22, 24, 27
NBA records 16
NBA Slam Dunk Contest 21, 27

P
Pettit, Bob **9**, 11, 12

R
Rivers, Glenn ("Doc") **20**, 21
Rock Island, Illinois 8
Rollins, Wayne ("Tree") 16, **17**, 18
Rookie of the Year Award 11
Roundfield, Dan 18, **19**

S
St. Louis, Missouri 8, 11, 12
Smith, Josh 27, 28, **30–31**
Smith, Steve 24, 27
Stoudemire, Salim 28

T
Tri-City Blackhawks 8
Turner, Ted 16

W
Webb, Anthony ("Spud") 21, **21**, 27, **27**
Wilkens, Lenny 12, 16, **16**, 24, 27
Wilkins, Dominique **4**, 5, 21, 22, **22**, **23**, 27, 28
Williams, Marvin 28, **29**
Willis, Kevin 21

DISCARDED LIBRARY BOOK

NOTTINGHAM ES, APS, VA

66816506   796. 323 LeB
The story of the Atlanta Hawks